Time Management and Profit Improvement

How to Work Less Hours and Make More Money

Table of Contents

Time management as a basis for a successful business
4 Strategic Time Step Management
Acquiring the Knowledge to Make Your Time Worth a Lot of Money
All you don't have to do for yourself, let someone else do
To your hours of quality and maximum upgrading
First of all, do a monthly/weekly management journal
Execution time as profitability and improvement
Profitability for Improvement of Tracks
This is how to do - raising prices
Outside outsourcing/construction team
Webinar, Conference, Workshop, Digital for Your Product Making Knowledge
you will save valuable time and automation technology
it's the most important! for yourself Sunsets

Time management as a basis for a successful business

Time is the most valuable and limited resource that we have. To succeed, we need a sophisticated and efficient time management system that will enable us to achieve our goals and dreams.

In recent years, I have accompanied dozens of business owners who have created impressive success stories, and one of the most exciting things I found was that the more entrepreneur
and business owner has managed his time, the more successful he is.

Sometimes the challenge is actually in successful people - the more you start to grow
in the business, the more customers and more business activity and the diary is filled with insanity, the
greater the difficulty of managing time. In contrast, people who are still unsuccessful in the business have a lot of time, and they do not always feel the challenge of time management, and as soon as they really start to take off and succeed in the business, new challenges arise, there are many more tAnd not many more things to do and then suddenly one big confusion is created. And not
do know who against whom and how to do everything.

You may by now have been alone in the business and now suddenly have a team, and if you have until now managed only yourself, now in addition to your headache
You need to manage all your staff and make sure everyone works properly, and suddenly you get to the point where you all find yourself Time managing the staff and constantly engaging in customer service for the benefit of the staff rather than promoting your

business.

To succeed in lifting your business to the next level, it's critical to managing time in the best possible way, which is why I found it appropriate to share with you guidance
this "Time Management and Profit Management".

In this booklet, we will discuss the most effective methods that will help you manage time
optimally so you can take off in your business.

Effective time management goes hand in hand with improving profitability, because my goal is to help you make your working time a maximum of money, so the question is not just how to manage time properly, but how to manage time right from a profitability perspective, and that's exactly your goal In this time management learning, you don't just want to know how to best organize your time, you want to sure
make you make the most of your time.

So come on, let's get going!

4 Steps to Strategic Time Management

There are four steps to strategic time management. These steps are arranged in chronological order and each stage is based on the previous step. We will go step by step
according to the pace of your progress in the business.

Step One: Acquire the knowledge and capabilities to make your time

worth a lot of money.

The first phase is the "beginner's phrase" - that's what I call it. Once we start building a business properly, well, first goal in
our terms of time management is to acquire the knowledge and capabilities to make time
our worth as much money as possible.

The more money you make from your time, the more time you're spent and your best utilized in terms of your output every hour. If today you have fifty earned dollars an hour and today you know how to make five
hundred dollars an hour, you created a multiplication times over the same working hour. If in the past it took you ten hours to make five hundred dollars, today one hour
makes you five hundred dollars - you created a very, very good time management.

The first phase goal is to acquire the knowledge and skills to know generate your time money. One of the things I focus on during my escort plans with business owners is: Increasing their profit per work hour. And we do that by building marketing machines and improving sales capacity. It can be through counseling that you can give and actually sell your time for high amounts, it can be any knowledge you have in mind - you can take that knowledge and leverage it in one form or another to make people pay you money for the knowledge you have acquired and gained Over the years, it can

be marketing writing, it can deal you do - a lot of
things you can do to make your time much more profitable.

At this stage - the first phase of the business starts, usually there is not much revenue and needle
many things done privately and independently. At this point, the entrepreneur is supposed to do
Everything on his own, and probably has no money for the secretary and the staff and employees. And then what happens is that he is very, very busy with
all the tasks and tasks he has
to do and so he has no time to turn around to
do the most important thing that is marketing. You see that in a lot of new business owners, all day long they
are only busy with current tasks because they do everything on their own and do not have time to turn around

marketing.

But the most important thing to remind them is that they must be focused on developing the marketing machine that will make them more money! Because a man who is busy from
morning to evening, finding the hot and the soulful to do everything in his business -
He runs to the bank and he runs here and he runs there, in the end, Today, if he doesn't invest in building a marketing machine that will make him more money per hour
, then he will remain stuck in this loop of technical work that most business owners
small are stuck with.

Eighty percent will invest twenty-eight. This is the principle of marketing and twenty percent do (the technical

80/20

endeavor

95%

or business owners do but most of the business. And

maybe five percent at best in marketing, making money - which is the most important thing to feed their business. They make treatment the main thing.

So if you are in this phase - in the first step, remember what is most important, that it is
marketing. True you have to do almost everything in business alone that still do not have a budget to staff or a secretary, but nevertheless, it is important to make sure that you

build and invest in the machine

development marketing machine, but

focused on

marketing, it will give you the light at the end of the tunnel, it frees you from The technical and frustrating marginalization will allow you to advance your business
to the next level.

Some people do not want to make a lot of money and it is good for them to make the five
thousand / ten thousand / fifteen thousand a month. They don't want to run employees,
They want to be an independent, private business, just
them and that's it. Completely legitimate for whoever is
his plan but remember there is no way
to make millions and become a private business - when you are alone with yourself. If you want to
stay in a small place and be a small, nice and kind business, then all the sections below that talk about employee management and team management are irrelevant to you because
you are not interested in it. But consider that you can't build a serious business, Certainly not a marketing asset - an asset that is worth your money if you don't create a team and if you don't create an entire set around you that helps you maximize what you
do with your time.

The first step in time management, which is the most important thing in starting a business, is

investing

to find the time to invest in developing a marketing machine.
The maximum, not in doing it but in marketing, so you can step out of this stage and move on to the next stage which is a lever for building a

much bigger and much more
significant business. Still here, if you are

in this situation that you are lonely, you have no employees, you have nothing and you do everything alone and you work and develop the marketing machine, you can still
do a lot to improve your time management.

Let's just start managing your email correctly, is it critical that you stay up all day working with your mailbox open? As long as you don't work full time in customer service, answering
customers, you should not do that. Even if you are engaged in customer service, you are not sure you have to be 100 percent constantly, you can open it every few hours and handle the incoming emails.

How long have you been on Facebook? This Facebook is a real one time saver!

Watsup - Do you always get notifications while you work? What happens is that we have a lot of distractions in the middle of the job that get us focused, get in the way of building activity
proper, a lot of things hinder us from maximizing our capabilities.
Let me tell you one thing about time: If you truly honor your time, you'll make a lot more money on your time.

I feel that one of the things that made me want to step forward and make more money on my work time and my time is because I started to respect my time more. If I respect my time, then I want to respect it, and those who do not respect
it will have a very difficult time pricing it respectfully.

So if you are constantly,
emailing watching or Facebook, you
Psychologically convince yourself that your time is unimportant, and if it doesn't matter, then obviously you can't
take a lot of money on it! You don't have to answer phones every day. Who said you must be on the phone with an open phone available twenty-four hours a day? Try turning off the phone for a few hours of work, concentrate, you will see suffice.
much more Even if you have customers, you can turn off the phone, you can find times that are unavailable so you can concentrate and invest your time best. (If you are in a situation that you really expect sales and sales phones and constantly have prospects on the line, then here I would say leave the phone open and open as much as possible.)

Because you are constantly checking emails, your business will not take off, you will be fine
on Facebook day, Business will not take off, as is WhatsApp, as are phones. Your business will
take off because of your time when you invest in business development, marketing development,
thought, thinking, strategy, planning, precise work.

People feel they work a lot, a lot, but in practice, they don't always work. You may have
office and you will be sitting there for
many hours, but that does not mean
that you are working at
those maximum.

I want to share with you today my theory, and my experience and a lot
of very successful business owners I see how they work and the direction is,
much less focus on responding to emails, Facebook, Watsup, phones, and more time
for thought, relaxation, planning, development.

Before I move you to the next level, it's important to emphasize that even if you are now in the first phase, you are just a small business and a beginner, the next steps are still

certain parts,

even if not everything is right for you today, that is

relevant to you!

You will exercise down the road, and you must understand and look at the full picture.
Even when you start a small business, you will look at it in terms of big business,
look at it with a big head and not a small head.

One of the things I find that differentiates successful people from people

less successful is the way of looking at business, who looks at his business big, strategically, broadly, he realizes that he is going to build a huge business and a huge
company, even if it takes time to reach the destination and fulfill his dream, he creates a CEO mentality and perspective, he looks at everything in the form of a serious company, so everything is built differently than someone who is still stuck in his small business and is in the loop, in his daily worries and he
don't even know how it will come out of it.

I would highly recommend you, even if you are in the first stage, to look forward and think
how Tam is going to build your business in a much more serious and wide way!
As I describe below.

Condensed first phase

Step Two: Everything you don't have to do yourself, let someone else

do!

This step is based on the implementation of the first phase. Which means you already
know how to make money of your time.

Execution of the first phase can be through hours of consulting, training

and Wiener, conference selling, sets you sell,

move, talk,

you

products you sell can be up-offer sales you learn to implement your store, and a variety of things that you already know how to do, and how to make the most of their
time, to make a lot of money And your de.

Once you've reached the second stage, where we want to talk about time management at another level
already.
At this point, your goal will be to shake off everything you don't have to, and let someone else do it. When properly trained, success often comes quickly. It may be that two months ago you were unsuccessful and suddenly today you are already making money, now your task will
be able to diagnose this thing where you
know how to make money from it and say: Okay, this is the thing I know how to do, this is the thing I know how to make five hundred, a thousand dollars, per hour.

But now what happens? You don't have many hours because your hours are occupied with all kinds of things that are less relevant, less critical and are not the things that make
you have money, but you have no choice, someone has to do it! And your goal here should be Everything you don't have to do, that someone else does!

You want to know what is best for you and what is the most effective way for you to make money and once you know what is the most effective way for you to make money, everything else you want to pass out. You don't want to be
stingy or frugal here and say, "
On the rope "or" The money on the rope "is the
waste, "because you have to understand that this time when you are busy with things you do not have to do
- It is a waste of money! It is the waste of
money you could make during those hours. (Again, if you have unlimited time and you do not know how to make money from your time, then it is clear that at least you will do all the tasks and do not lose
money to let someone else do when you don't make money).

Here's an example: Suppose you know how to give advice and you have clients who come in, pay you five hundred dollars for each hour of

counseling, (a lot of my students in advanced "Commando members" programs charge dollar 500-2,000 for
counseling) a hundred hours a month They'll make you fifty thousand dollars . But if you don't do a hundred hours, you only do fifty hours, because another fifty hours you get stuck on other things, you only get twenty-five thousand
dollars, so you want to move everything you don't have to. It can be outsourcing, it can be freelancing (actually letting someone, an outside vendor, do the work for you), it can be a team of employees you hire, for example - if you want or need to build a website, you might know how to build a website and you've done it before, but maybe the time it takes you, it's ten hours and ten hours of work that you can give advice at seven hundred fifty dollars an hour, that's seven thousand five
hundred dollars ! So if someone else does it for you - thirty hours at $ 4,000, it would be much smarter than selling your time cheap.

It could be giving someone external management of
the campaign is financed
on Facebook or just manage your
Facebook page,
or dose service,
customer or even make sales, (although the first stage would recommend to everyone to make sales on their own, but if down the road if you can do things you earn them more money than your current sales, you will pass sales to someone else.)

You constantly want to check what your hourly rate is or how much an hour is worth in real-time. Even if you are not consultants but if you can produce a package and sell it for five thousand dollars, it takes you to produce the package in ten hours. So you can make five hundred dollars an hour, and if I am

marginal to your agenda, you can produce and sell

now download
such packages.

For example, if you need a graphic design for one of your products, and suppose you
know how to design great, but it will take you much longer than graphic designer
an experienced, let a graphic designer do it for a few bucks. Your time is more important.

Another example, let's say you're running a conference. You can come early before the
event and put in all the prospects, edit and arrange the refreshments and do it all by yourself, or have someone who can do some of the work for you, be it your employee or an outside producer who will save you this mess with

the marginal things. If you handle the paperwork and need to take it out of the print shop, you can pay someone to run for you. Someone can run to the bank for you, it can even be at the level of a house cleaner, a brewery, someone to do some shopping for you, anything you don't have to do and you do, it's at your expense! Nothing
to do, our hours are limited.

that it was I concluded.
I am preparing Weekend, (I used to do every Friday Chicken), this time cost me
three thousand five hundred dollars.
So if it's my fun to make the
chicken (and from time to time it's my fun), then I'll make it. But if it's not my fun and it catches my time, then isn't it a waste of time? At three thousand five hundred
dollars I can get someone to cook for me from morning to evening, every week!

Of course when there are things you can do, so it's part of your pleasure to do them and you don't have to give them up, but the idea is that your time will be available for the really important things and not for all kinds of technical arrangements you can
give others to do.

So if you are a consultant who is taking on advice even just one hundred and fifty dollars an hour, and you now want to go clean the house. A cleaner

will take you sixty dollars an hour. Do the calculation: Isn't it worth giving a consulting hour now
and taking a hundred and fifty dollars and financing three hours of cleaning at your place?

You should look at everything you do daily and think: What else someone can do for me with less money?

You want to do the calculation consistently, how much your profit will be realized in real terms and what you do today and how you manage your time best. It's your biggest goal, anything you don't have to do, not critical that you do, that someone else knows and can do it and can be trained to do it, that it does. You will invest your time in it
developing and promoting business.

What happens in an advanced business?
Let's talk about an advanced business. This is stage two-plus. Once you have a business and you have a team, you can also go up another step and appoint managers under you so they manage the team. You can take the CEO to manage the team, it can also just be a shift manager.

Suppose you have three employees working for you in the office, you can take the best, pay him a little more money and tell him, "You run the shift, "Or" You manage a client portfolio, all customers will contact you and not me "and you
with this move can move
forward and invest your time in marketing to bring more
and more customers into the business.

Example: One of the clients VIP ran an office services business (Outsourced office.) Every day she had to talk to existing customers and take care of her employees and she did not have time to bring new clients into the business and promote her business. I told her: Come take a shift manager who will only be in regular contact with the customers daily and will also be in charge of your employees
and you will be able to move on and develop the business. Once she did,

her business progressed and evolved significantly. This stage of the appointment of managers below you is a more advanced level course of business when you have money not only employees but also someone to manage them
and guide them.

There is also the topic of sales training. You may not be the best people to manage and mentor the team, so let's get the right people to mentor and run your team so that your time is managed
best.

By the way, this is the model I applied to my American course company, I took my best employee and promoted her to the CEO to run the company. "I asked the second-best employee to be my VP and she runs all employee management activities. The management team managed through two CEO mine and it
fear me and allow me
to do the best I can
know and like to do in my time, and be responsible for things these (which are very important
to the business, but not crucial that I
personally will do the same.)

set Regular times for staff management and answering their questions
I'll give you another tip about employee management. To manage the employees in your way
Correct, you need to set times to manage the team and answer their questions. If you are sitting in the office, the door of your open every second entered the work or works differently to ask you questions or give you phones without end, you
Life does not succeed to move forward, you will be all day busy Blhdric them, help them, help them and answer the questions in there and you do not make progress any
Anywhere, any time will you diversion opinion.

So you want to allocate time for questions and tell workers: two to ten to one - then I answer all the questions your. In other words, do n't bother me all
This morning.

After you have done it, have you the hours of work of your morning - vacancies.
Until the time two often in the afternoon you close the door, enter the bunker
And begin to work, concentrate at work, otherwise you will not be enough to do anything. If the team of your need guidance, there is no problem, if not enough for two to ten to
One, so one of the days of the week, you will do the training and guide them,
Will determine one day in the morning to meet the team, you do sitting of time - two hours and sit with the team of your, but not all the time you service team that then
Not succeed in work, do not succeed in advance!

You must produce concentration, must produce a schedule that you really will work and not work in the wrong - take the bit of time left for you after all distractions
And to dedicate it to work, really not.

I'll give you an example of a found favor in my eyes, showing how phase two -
Means to shake what you do not have to do and get employees to manage the
Book your right - is all that critical business size and growing. One of the clients of my have had meetings recognizes that work very well and is selling pretty highly. Known as the marketing of his is to invite people to a meeting, the meeting is selling packs pretty worth $ 18,000 that " millions per package. In one of the meetings of ours is sharing with me that he wants to do even conference familiarity which he would sell the parcels to his. There has been called one called " meetings " and he wants to build a machine again called " conference sales," later he came to me and said to me: " I want
Also, do a digital course to get me more clients. "

But what's his problem? There has referred one that works well, is called a second he wants to do now is come to me with a machine Thirdly, and during our meeting shared it turns out the problem is true of his is in general not known as article marketing, there has referred
Great that works well! His problem is that he ca n't give any more output
Three customers new month, that he does everything alone business, and is not

More than three customers.

to take

successful

He comes to me at the height of energy and thinks the solution to his problem is to do a conference and digital course, and what will happen? I shot from another lot a very long time to build the course, I shot from time to market the course and at the end of the day what is the course that will give him? Bring him, customers who lack it, that is
I already know how to make appointments that work well. This machine of meetings works for him and the machine of the conference will also work for him, he
No more marketing machine needed! It should produce volume engine, and the ability to manufacture more
High and its only way is to take employees.

I told him: Employees in your will to all things technical that you do, that It can teach each one! What you will do is just sit down and make your appointments
Sale and sell the packages, because it employees your not able to do, that
They never had the plan sales My nor have the knowledge that you have. But if you are
Keep all the time to do them all alone, all the machines marketing news
You are trying to do, you will not help, you will not solve the problem.

This example amazing how sometimes you think that should make a machine and the machine is not the problem of your, but need to improve the capacity engine of the machine
Existing, the production capacity. In the case of a client in the - VIP Mine, just had to
Manage the time his true through work further to allow him to enter

Ten customers each month.

Another example: This is what happened with another client of mine, who is currently very switched
Serious.

When she came to me initially at first, she was doing branding itself
No employees and she took ten thousand dollars on branding which was nice
For her, though, it took her a whole month of work to do the branding. Once she built the marketing machine as I instructed her and she created
A well- known Webinar and an exposure conference during which it sells the branding packages and raised the price of a branding package from ten thousand dollars to thirty
And fifty thousand dollars, now has she been called, and the time of her she will utilize in the best to maintain the machine that - do Wiener, conference, bringing customers in and talk to you, else it sits with them to meetings and to sell the
The packages.
To it, even one another is not the know to do but to do practice their branding
And the graphic design she doesn't have to bother with, she can pay some money
Graphic artists who will come and work for her. And just within a few months she opened an office, took two graphic artists to work

She had a full -time job, plus a secretary, and suddenly found she could easily make a hundred thousand dollars a month. Two transactions of fifty thousand dollars, it's a hundred thousand
Dollar. Three deals is one hundred and fifty thousand dollars. Or she closes three
Transactions of thirty -two thousand dollars, this ninety thousand dollars. So it's true that the graphic artist will cost her between eight thousand a month or seven thousand a month or some that the graphic artist pays. So what happened? So she paid the amount that now she can spend the whole day in her activity Marketing. Where most
Her day was stuck in graphic design, and most of her day turned to marketing.

Then again, I return you to the section first, at first until there she is called, is not can finance graphic artist and office, that really does not have money for salaries and more do not know to make money , but at the moment who knows how to make money, you invest in your marketing and all activity around - You will find employees who will
The everything for you in great.

Step Three - maximizing and upgrading the quality of the hours your

Let's move on to the third phase of strategic time management. If at first, we know how to make money from the time of the work our, Phase II is to take care to have us a few more hours like this, that we cleared the whole things are not relevant laced " g our then offer right away we have a lot of hours that we can
Do them a lot of very
Money. We are now moving forward
And move on to the third stage,
Which is enchanting and upgrading
The quality of your hours.

Let's become honest: you can work five hours, but some time from hours of those you concentrated work? On the job, you work
Eight hours Let's say, how long do you work?
Most owners of businesses do not manage to work all
Time. They are not concentrated, there are none
They have energies, there are a million and one reasons why they don't do the job like
Properly.

On the other hand, if you look at it thoroughly, you will find that you have effective hours And you sufficient them a lot, and compared it there you hours that you are not enough
There is nothing in them and you feel stuck in the place, with no progress. And because you are independent and there you boss over your head, then you can also more easily

Drift and take advantage of the time, compared to an employee who has a boss who sits him on the head and tail and not let him quit
To work. But what you must remember that at the end of the day business is your own, then you are the bosses of yourself and you want
Derive the maximum hours of work in your, therefore, step that aims to make every hour of your hourly much more quality, time of creativity, of inspiration, of ideas. Sometimes one idea can bounce you off
Business but in everyday life do you the time to think about and succeed right. So you want to improve your time to you, the quality of the hours you're using energy positive, motivated and quiet, so you get inspiration and power bumps the

Your business.

What I want to ask you, it's basically: What helps you to concentrate and succeed in the most effective? What are the things that help you concentrate and produce a very, very high-quality hour? What is it that will help with the effectiveness of working hours
Yours? It can be a release, freedom, sleeping, reading, playing, sports, walking, jogging daily, skiing, sailing, cycling, Exit nature, beach sea, forest, scenery, events social, tours, visits to places of interest, restaurant good, Departure
Spousal, family, disengagement from daily stress, prayer, meditation, Retreat, every one of you to take it to where
He wants to take the this, but what those are producing the ideas inspiring inspiration
Greatest efficient.

When you sit for eight hours in the office and working, the output of your having business would be less good than if you take breaks and releases to be filled
In energies. Of course, if you are working in the company as employees and tell the boss your " I want to now go out to sea to concentrate," he was throwing you all the steps that have room for one company mission that brings ideas and this role
Of the boss. But because you are self-employed, you are those who have to come up with ideas, with creativity , you need to come up with a product of your, with selling your own, think about machine marketing Otherwise you can do to improve , and you do to it a lot more good on the shore of the sea or a slope ski or boat or in a hotel or on a trip , or through release stress through will produce
You have positive energies, motivation, and a completely different mindset.

Robin Sharma, author of multi- Sale
" The monk who sold his Ferrari in his, " writes: " I make the most money

"(Wisdom)

Mine on the ski slope, "
Excellence) "

I all so love the book that the wisdom of excellence, that this collection

and all

Great

Of ideas

whole

Idea I say to my wife: "Ashley,

Robin Sharma

Right well I would write to it just
Like that? "

And that 's it, he saved me the time to write a book. If you want to know the thinking of my, read the " wisdom of excellence ." A lot of thinking mine and a description of mine are there in the book of this and it's nice because actually, it encourages me
I think in the right direction. So here is what Robin Sharma writes in the book: " I get the big ideas

Most of my, your thoughts to lift the business of me and brought about a revolution
My life when I'm relaxed and enjoying life, sometimes often I was joking with my listeners
When I say that I am making the most money in my on the slope skiing, people are smiling,
But they understand the point of mine. "
Should contact the place to let the genius of your login. So you want to
Produce effective time, make the
The time in your hour of energy, an hour full of inspiration, while full of creativity, as the head of your open. So look
The thing that makes you to it and invest in it, maybe it is more talk of,

But should you do it?

You will find that the time you go for a swim in the morning will do wonders for your business. True, you take off time for work to swim, but three hours remain for you, will be the results of a lot more good than four hours were you before yes when you came
Tired and exhausted trying to sit down and write an email, then take this account.

I, for example, one of the tools as good of writing marketing it just to make active physically. I'm going for a swim, coming back from swimming, and immediately I wrote an email within several minutes, where it would take me three hours because I got stuck and advanced with
The writing, because the head is tired, the head is drained.

C, John Carlton, one of the copywriters as well in saying that there have two tips
For good marketing writing, one tip is to sleep well at night, sleep eight hours
Plus, the other tip is to take a refreshing shower ...

If no you long for things these will inspire you, get
That you are probably investing in things that are not critical to invest in.
Now look, part of the success in life is to say "no," to refuse

For things and projects that don't promote you directly. Could be that you are very outgoing and very popular and invite you all today to be interviewed on the radio, television, events, conferences and you're running from place to place , that the Ten Commandments in your message : " duty to go to any place who you " and you're wasting time very very expensive , and investors regarding the most important
For you, this is a fundamental focus of business development.

If you download a parade today to all the things that promote your business, You will find that you have plenty of time! And part of the time that you invest at three, managing time effectively, which is to make the time your more convenience and, in this
Means taking vacations, yes, that means stopping, letting the business plummet for three days,
It 's okay, while that fill up with energy and come in new and fly forward. Ideas as well in my business are not formed on the slope ski ... but created

That I take

Small

On holidays

To myself. It can be a little freedom
Right, or all sorts of things
Little ones I do that are just there
My big ideas are formed. I can tell you what the business idea came to me when I was in some
Tel Aviv hotel, what's the idea
That I came from vacationing on the Sea of Galilee, and when I was in California what idea I came up with and what experiment I brought from there, and when I was
In Italy, what is the business idea I came up with there? Every time I went to some resort, got some insight into the business, although it took time to implement her business, but the insight that made me a lot of very money and was worth the few days when not working (but of course you want to create a situation
That your business will work even if you are not there for three-four days)
...
I want to encourage and encourage you, take this time for yourself ...

To invest in a good best for yourselves, so time you really would be a lot more quality. At the end of the day, you are working with mind your own, with a mind of your, not with eight hours of work at the office. You are the ones who have to bring ideas. If you sit in the office and look at the walls, or in front of the computer, they will not come
From there great ideas ...

Step Four - Manage calendar week/month do you order at the top

Let's move forward on phase IV managing time effectively, it is managing log weekly - monthly. Until now basically was the preparation, now you take the whole it and put it into a log neat arranges you your assignments By time.
Let us build a log monthly and it 'll have the ingredients below :
1. The component of action
Calendar first of all to the - 20% of the work, (the way all this, 50% sadly .)
All the things that choice and must do - you have to do. You sold guiding parents, then you need to sit down and do practice the guidance of parents This one. You sold advice, then you need to sit down and do practice the consultation.

I joke with my clients as I sit with them

I'm sitting with you

To them: " It is

In meetings and I say

Now, it's within the framework of the - 20% of the mine, that I have no choice , I have to do because you paid me a lot of money and I must deliver you the goods and give you the time to mine, but it's not the - 80% develops me the business . "
Although I really could calculate the hours of consulting my
As part of the 80% of marketing because the job is only my all consultations, courses, and programs to escort mine is to produce successful non- profit for clients of my tales success in provoking inspiration, I believe Scshlkohot My succeed in an ordinary and multiply the business of their This activity Marketing
The best for me.

So, first of all, we put in the diary the things that have no choice, we must do. But you must make sure that it does not grab you the whole diary that if it grabs you the whole diary, something here screwed up completely, and you will not succeed lift
Business.

You have to make sure it's not eighty percent. It can be or fifty percent
Or twenty percent or thirty, but the main thing is that you have time to do more things.
Remember! This time of doing is not what makes you new money.

2. Time Weekly planning and thinking strategically
Other income the component activity log, you want to put in the time Week
For strategic planning and thinking.
Whether you do the planning
And thinking this through Counseling
Business you get in between
You make it yourself alone, a must to invest time weekly
For weekly thinking and planning. It may also be you sitting

The couple, with the partner

Or daughter

With a son

And think and build the program weekly and monthly of what you are going to do this week in business. You want to put the time of planning and thinking into that journal
Otherwise, it won't happen!

3. Time for training and team management
If there is you people Sales Sometimes suddenly things begin to creak and work as needed, so you put in the diary long special, let's say on Monday that
Do a three-hour training for the team. It does not have to be every day, every week, but need to decide when you are doing the this
And put in the diary so that it does happen.

4. Time to work on this month's campaigns
The next task we will put in the diary is time to work on the marketing campaigns of

This month - the fixed and basic things. Let's say you do a monthly webinar or
Conference months, then you want to put before all the things. I call it " our bread and meat," it's the food that makes your business tick, which is your company 's main revenue. So if you have you something permanent, known as article marketing you do, you run it every month again, you want
First of all, make sure that it works as needed.

5. Prioritize among all the other projects that remain
Beyond all things incomes calendar, you must do things more
And now to continue to grow the business.
So what you want to do this is prioritization of all projects that remain to you then
Divide them either by weeks or by months. That said, could be that you have a lot of projects not be enough this month to put everything log, so you decide how you divide you're it on over
The months - what goes into February, what March, what April, what June, what July,
But at least you 'll know the face of each year how to project your spread.

Let's say you want to improve an existing system, - (suddenly you tell yourself :
"Ioao, course mine is not good, I must replicate the lesson number two of course.)" Could be that you say: " I want to project a new," " I want to make another campaign, more active marketing," maybe that you want to write a book, maybe you want to do some water large, can be
That you want to improve the series of emails that customers receive after the Webinar,

You want to produce Afsiil, you want to produce the product the second fifth and tenth, maybe you want to produce Wiener style else, maybe you want to do a conference, you want to plan the continuation customers your, you want to do
Club - there are lots of things you want to do and there is no situation that you do all month, so if you do not insert this diary in a precise, this
It will not happen! For example, if you want to write a book, you put in an hour - two hours
Week to start work on the book. Then, true, it will take a year or two, but at least you started

Work on it. You can say: I want to take four, five hours, to improve the rate of two a course mine, and I need to end up with this fast, so you play the Diary and say: Okay, it's true this month
We are not, we can get everything, but what
Made this month will be work on
Asia and improve the rate of several

They are the stuff

Because they asked

Two,

Most important to me right now, in the month
Next, we will start to work on more things.

This is what is called prioritization. You must stop and decide what is most critical, what is most profitable, what is most important for the business, and put it into the journal's priority. Journal Your must be conducted in all things these are defined and marked face, if you do not define, the end does not remain you time things most important , you 'll be stuck element of action and perhaps a maximum Another tip slightly beyond , and things will turn out and you do not you can really invest in activities that are really

Critical to the business you will be growing all the time!

The extract of the fourth phase

Let's do an intermediate summary and we will go over the four steps to time management briefly :

1. step first managing time: lets you learn, you will gain the abilities of your gain
Maximum money from your time, from your work time.

2. The second step in time management: After you already know how to make money, you want to
Turn a few more hours in Hello ׳ m your things important really and move
Everything you do not have to do, out, etc. , to someone else.
3. The third step in time management: You improve the quality of your work time,
To make you much more productive and much more efficient. When you sell
Something very important to get on sale with energies. If you do not come with energy, the deal will not close. So it is very critical if you come from tired screams
And frustrated or you come with peak energy. 4. Phase IV management time: take all steps preceding and begin to build the calendar. Enter the part of the work that must be done the same, the time weekly
For planning and strategic thinking for the business, the time for training and team management, the time
Work on the campaigns of the month and then make a prioritization of all the other projects
Remaining.

I want to give you an example of the implementation of the four stages in business :
Let׳s say you have a store. What will you put in a journal? How will you arrange it? Action is: ordering merchandise, handling suppliers, accounts of banks, deposit checks, designing the store, organize the goods, all the things these can catch
You the whole day, but it׳s only a component of action! You must make sure left you time to train the personnel sales selling
Shop, sit with them, to explain to them how to makeup - Ciel, how to smile at customers, what is the culture and values of the store and the business of our, you have to devote time to write your ads advertising your month near the newspaper, you want time

Write the messages by email ״ to, you want to design them, and it will not happen if you wait all day for that day, it might happen, you have to put the whole diary. You also want time to plan monthly campaigns. All things these take time and you put your all log in neat, so you
Make sure that you doing it.

Let's become real, not always we stand destinations in the calendar our, but at least
Bring your maximum capacities!

Improving and increasing profitability

Improving profitability is out of managing the time we talked until now about managing time. But managing time communicating automatically improve profitability because the meaning of management time is to make the most out of every hour of work. That's why I found it appropriate to add the recommended routes here as well
To improve profitability.

In the business to succeed For people who are already getting started Designed for advanced,
That part Theirs.
Suppose I do consultations and I earn a lot of very money the time of consultation , but today my limited and run out of hours work , I never could get more clients and then does not have the possibility to improve further the profitability mine, so maybe I 'll pass on preparing Chicken on Friday and then I turn myself more time for work, okay, but what Moving on?

So there are four tracks that I want you to meet, be aware of them
And work with them to improve the profitability of your.
The first track is raising prices, the second track is team building and outsourcing
Except, track third is to make the knowledge of your product Digital All it: Workshop, Wiener, conference or format to another of one of the lots and the track IV is
Automation and use of technology to save time.

Let's get to the depth of these four tracks...

4 tracks to improve profitability

Route 1 - raising prices

To increase profitability is The first route Prices.

There are some things you need to do to succeed
Raise prices :

Look into the eyes of the customer

Courage
Courage and self- confidence.

And tell him the price you think you deserve.

That proves the advice

Success stories
Look at the customer potential the stories of success your

Your, product your own, really worth the price you require.

Packing again
Suppose instead of selling advice per hour (where customers pay according to the tariff hourly
You're) sell the This package designed advice. Not selling hours, but selling a topic.
For example, I have a client who sells Internet infrastructure. He doesn't sell working hours,
He sells a package that is infrastructure. Then maybe it takes him five hours to do the infrastructures of these, but it can take on this twenty thousand dollars. This is how you earn a lot
More per hour! Another example: Suppose you have a self- defense course and that requires six sessions that you come and teach self- defense. So instead of saying: I am taking the time twenty -five dollars and sell six hours those hundred and fifty dollars, you can
Say: I am selling the program the full protection of self in two hundred fifty dollars, then, true that the program is six hours, but the measurement is not per hour, is bull

Plan! The same thing you can do branding, you are the familiar package of branding, I'm not a writer, some costs me all Rolf and some costs me all of pliers, or some costs me time
Work, but I get the whole package or buy a marketing array! We can
Pack the service of our re. Of course, if you are a business that sells physical products, you will have a lot
Difficult to raise prices of
The physical products in the store when they are sold in the fort store at a certain price, but the way to do so
Succeed at it, it's to sell comparable products. As would you store more products that are in the stores of the other, you can pack them
A more than good. Matter of packaging reconnected also packs internet, also stores, as well
For consulting packages.
Almost everything you sell, if you pack it again in another,
You can raise the prices.

Proof of utility
Of course, to raise the prices you should also prove beneficial, some

The service/product of your worth for the customer . As you can see the customer how much worth it what you give him so that he would be happy to pay
More money on it. And, of course, that the most important, it Tacheles be quality ! Give the customer something that solves problems. At the end of the day they lie as good this truth and at the end of the day you can fool some of the people some of the time, somewhere you can fool all
Time to all the people and sell them something that is not good. You can sell, make a sale, sell what something screwed up and maybe do Coupe small, but long- term, if you want to be a business fails, it is not
Effective.

Think strategically, will be the best in what you do, sell the thing best of the best, the thing quality best, give an experience that no one else will not give you will find some easy it raise the prices
Through this thing. As you will be better quality, more real, so
You will succeed in raising prices.

I want to give you an example of my tariff route.
How I'm I raised the tariffs for consultation mine?
I started with five hundred dollars an hour, after this , it came to a thousand dollars an hour, after it increased to two thousand dollars an hour, after this in an elegant told the two thousand plus VAT " than , that two thousand three hundred forty and after it took the two thousand three hundred forty and I plus VAT " M, that is two thousand seven hundred thirty
And seven and after it took more time to two thousand seven hundred thirty -seven, I plus VAT " from and it turned to be three thousand two hundred and then decided
Possible round this thousand dollars. It's a track raising prices My, and how only I could do the
This is through the elements I showed you earlier.

So let's summarize again the elements are: It is courage, stories of success, this pack it packages, this proves useful and that provides a solution to a genuine and quality. Then the client says: "Listen, I invest a thousand dollars in consulting time, but it's worth it to me
Two thousand or three thousand, so really this investment great. "

That's what you want! You want customers to you will feel they are investing in you the investment the best they can invest, and when they feel the
This, you will bring forth on the price of yours. All further investment is still attractive and good, you succeed in raising the

Prices.

Point important about raising prices: Some people have problems with mental and emotional problems with raising rates, they feel bad to raise prices. To people like that I say, "Look, it's for the benefit of the customers that you're raising prices because you can give your maximum for the benefit of the customer, you can invest in the quality of the product you Give the customer, the quality of service you provide to the customer."

For example, my, this is so. Look, people pay me a lot of money for advice, As you know, one of the most expensive in Israel, but take into account that it allows me
Come and spend even myself and take consultations and ideas of the people best the best in the world, people who I can pay for if not I height amounts significantly
About my advice. One of the mentors of my overseas " to paying a hundred and twenty thousand dollars on meeting advice of several hours. So do not fall off the chair, but the way my stand it is because I take the amounts that I think come to me, I take expensive and it can give me the knowledge quality best that exists around the world and bring it
To you - to my clients. If I download you a price and then never was able to take the training and qualifications of the best in the world, so also you would get the quality of a lot less good. So at the end of the day, you do a very big favor to your customers when you invest in quality and when you take a lot of money from them. And those who want
Purchase cheap can go to your students.

Route 2 - building a team/sourcing foreign

Let's talk about the track next, which is to build a team of sourcing outside or team. People say, " I'm an expert on relationships, how do I get a team to

do the job? I'm the one who needs to sit down and do the consultations ." So let's think, maybe take mentors
In your method that they do the consultations?

Suppose people agree to pay you five hundred dollars s for consulting your topic parity, log your fill up and at the end of the day and will remain you a lot of time for the provision of further consultations , so what you can make it do a course for students your , produce you students , mentors method in your and now you sell the guidance of mentors in your and it will not grab just the time your own ! Have you much more time, that part of the work goes mentors and advisors working method to yours. So if I have a total of twenty hours of counseling, but I have five
Mentors, I turned the twenty into a hundred hours of counseling.

You can also recruit employees who can do part or all of the work,
A team that can solve problems, customer service, salespeople.
It tracks the other allows you to improve the profitability of your, that at the end of the day some govern the time
Your, time you're limited.

Route 3 - Transform your knowledge into a digital product/workshop/conference/webinar

Golf Tuesday to improve profitability is: make the knowledge of your product Digital, workshop, Wiener, conference or anyway otherwise you can sell at a much
People. Here I want to show you some routes you take Please note, members of the " Commando " mine use in processes these successful very important
Have you head in neat how the process of this work.

A. One by one - for a course or frontal workshop
The first step is to go from personal counseling - you give one- to- one to the client,
For a course or frontal workshop.

Today I take one hour

Example :

And doing consulting five hundred dollars, if I sit down and do a course of ten or twenty people, and each one will pay me only one hundred dollars Sea, will have two thousand dollars an hour instead of five hundred dollars per hour. So it takes the one on one and make
Same for a course or frontal workshop.

This is to move from a frontal course to a course

B. Course Frontal - Course Digital Live
Stage next to your order to maximize profit, Digital Live, which not requires the customer to your life in the same area as yours. Because if you have a workshop
Frontal in the " Hope " neighborhood, customers from other cities can not reach you, because what to do, this

A piece of travel. But as soon as you move it's digital, it Leib, it's interactive, you make it all day at two in ten in the morning or seven

In the evening or nine in the evening each week. So it's still a course, but you allow people
All the world to join and you increase the revenue of yours!

C. Course Digital Live - Course Digital recorded or edited physical
The next step will be: Instead of a Digital Live course, let's do something pre-recorded
Or a set of physical and we would save us hours of work. Suppose there you have a course of eight hours, eight meetings and you sold it, you now need to provide the whole eight hours. Get out of the house for eight nights

And give the lectures and activities

Or Arabs
Yours.

But if you do this form is recorded in advance, or the set of physical or digital, have saved you the whole eight hours of these, eight weeks, eight Days when you can do another marketing activity.

Example: Client mine named Moshe Stern, in a commando, is involved under the guidance of parents and is recognized at the conference the package of his that includes eight sessions loaders. So instead of doing a conference and sell eight meetings two weeks, it was eight weeks, which is jammed with customers, he can sell at a conference the course is digital in his or physical in his (edited physically the materials) and then left him eight
Weeks where every evening he can make conference another group differently and sell again,
And so it doubles the results of his according eight!
True, there is a situation because the course is digital, buy him a little less people, but still, it's the results of in accordance five, according to the six, it is still a growth of five hundred
Percentage of time management!

D. From personal counseling to group counseling
Step further is to take advice personally and make it a consultation group.

So you can actually borrow one- on- one, and you can borrow one- on- many, or even do a little conference. Suppose there you conference smaller of thirty people and every time you bring thirty people to convene, then simply place get three conferences, you can make a conference one with many more participants than have to you one hundred customers that you are taking care of them at the same time. (Except for cases where there

Why

Strategies

You have reasons

Format

Insert

You do the

Small and boutique and worth you go
And make it three times .)

Now, take into account that when you take advice personally and turn it into a group or taking one on one
And say to him: " Come on course," " Come to the group," you must sweeten the pill to the customer, give him compensation and create a situation of " WIN-WIN" I mean
That you win because you save time, but also is a winner and earn something.
And how do you make it?
You have to think and build something really powerful which leaves that client
Gets more and you get more. You get more - it's understandable why you save time that can make you a lot of money, but let's create a situation that the customer also
He'll earn a lot more in the team than he would if you sat one- on- one with you.

How did I make it? You ask? I gave the members of the " Commando " My seminar sales at the hotel for two days including the cost of the hotel, including everything, gave them a seminar More of writing marketing at the hotel for two days, I answer personal email, What's Up, and sometimes even phone. I also winners where you can ask questions and the answers, I also developing capabilities consultancy business and created a situation of winning - winning, even they earn all that much, and
I optimize the management of time in my - a lot of the time my free stuff really
Important, rather than sit down and pluck the
Head hairs with customers one on one!

Group

About quality

I am very careful

That the group

Mine and be careful

The " Commando "

Stay small and high-quality and that your friends

In the past

there were

Get attitude and responding personally,

People who wanted to join and simply turned them in programs and things other to keep the group of the " Commando " quality and small. Some of the applicants received service
Marketing staff of my making them the marketing, part found solutions to other,
But I insisted on always maintain the character and quality to the highest of the group .)

You want to do it too, you want to meet the obligations you to customers. Therefore it is important really will produce a solution with compensation for a good customer, compensation for such
It will be worth it and it will also benefit from it and then you will succeed in the long run!

Route 4 - Automation and technology that will save you valuable time

Track IV is, using automation and technology to save time. Each of us does a lot of things, and there are actions we do manually but possible
Do them in a much more professional way
And fast and automatic.

For example, you can schedule the whole
The weekly and monthly emails
Your advance, you can schedule Facebook to all posts in your

Pre week ahead, if you put in a customer-client in a manual for your own, you can find some software that makes it for you. There are loads

And then you just are

Things that can be done using technology and save time.
I can earn much more in your time!

The essence of the fourth track

Summary of the 4 Tracks for Improving Profitability :
Let's summarize the four paths to improve profitability,
In the first track: We will invest in raising prices through proper packaging, Courage, a good and powerful response for the customer . Track II: Build a team and people who can do the work or parts of it for you, to maximize what you do. Take into account that if there is your line you want to take out into the world, if you will train mentors for them to pass it on the news, you can reach out and touch many more people than if you try
Make it all by yourself alone. Track III: check whether there is something; Product, know that you can make one on one - one of the many or through maximizing the knowledge your . (Sometimes Do not you know and the thing that is not relevant to you, not all one must do
Course or webinar). The fourth route: to check what can be done in automation, in what technology
It can be used to save time.
These are the four fast track to improving your profitability.

Invest in yourself!

In conclusion, I would like to remind you to spend on the important most, That you are yourselves!

You must make time to read books. What books? You decide. I recommend you to book biographies, books management

Read books, you will

You want to be good at marketing,

And marketing. If

Looking at the broader more about how the world looks, you will learn the founders of Google, Larry Page,
And Sergey Brin who share the ideas
Their, you will learn Meg, Jeff Bezos founder of Amazon,

Starbucks, you learn

Founder

You will learn

Elon Musk Tesla and Phil Knight Founder

Companies that wrote

administrative

Nike and all kinds

Books and give the ideas of the largest in their management of business management employees
And time management. And if you tell me: life does us time to read
Books, so you'll understand you're in trouble!

Sometimes you want to read a book to
To be released, it has been associated with what we discussed earlier: how to improve the time your through reading good and liberation, but here I am talking about reading books that allow you to continue to be good because you
I want to be the best most.

You want to create a continuation of learning constantly. It can be more courses, more things to promote you, it can be to continue to develop the knowledge of your profession
Yours - For example, if you are a couples consultant, then continue to learn more about couples counseling.

I believe that a consultant double as good in the world and adviser Double half of it, but if Attorney
The less good, more good than the first marketing, the second win of course and puts more money.

Say, is it not preferable to be also one marketing best of the best in the area you and nobody professionals best most field yours? You will be also an adviser to the couple as well, that knows the best market or adviser to instruct as well also know as a good market, or
Reflexologists are as good as even know the best market.

Take your all, you invest even the quality of your and knowledge your and knowledge of marketing your own, knowledge of business your own, so really you will achieve more time
Yours.
Invest time to surround his people better,

Invest time development capabilities professionalism,

Professional,

Advice

BlackBall

Invest

Marketing capabilities, all these things are very, very important and they are Things will advance and will propel the business to yours!

Hope production of the benefit with the counseling committed to your success

www.ingramcontent.com/pod-product-compliance
Lightning Source LLC
Chambersburg PA
CBHW030542220526
45463CB00007B/2950